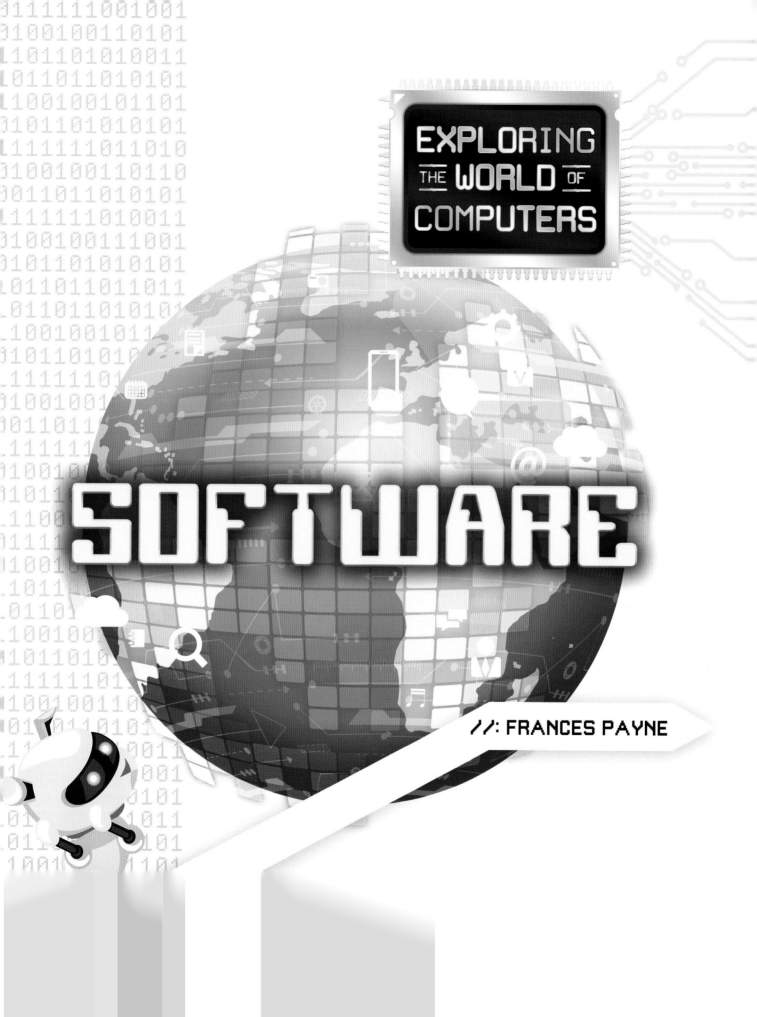

EXPLORING THE WORLD OF COMPUTERS

SOFTWARE

// FRANCES PAYNE

Redback Publishing
PO Box 357 Frenchs Forest NSW 2086
Australia

www.redbackpublishing.com
orders@redbackpublishing.com

© Redback Publishing 2020

ISBN 978-1-925860-73-3

Author: Frances Payne
Editor: Marianne Lindsell
Designer: Redback Publishing

Original illustrations © Redback Publishing 2020
Originated by Redback Publishing

Printed and bound in China

Acknowledgements
Abbreviations: l—left, r—right, b—bottom, t—top, c—centre, m—middle
We would like to thank the following for permission to reproduce photographs: (Images © shutterstock)
p20tl By Aleksandra Suzi,

Every effort has been made to contact copyright holders of any material reproduced in this book. Any omissions will be rectified in subsequent printings if notice is given to the publisher.

Disclaimer
All the internet addresses (URLs) given in this book were valid at the time of going to press. However, due to the dynamic nature of the internet, some addresses may have changed, or sites may have changed or ceased to exist since publication. While the author and publisher regret any inconvenience this may cause readers, no responsibility for any such changes can be accepted by either the author or the publisher.

MIX
Paper from
responsible sources
FSC® C020056

A catalogue record for this book is available from the National Library of Australia

Contents

Computer Software

Computer software includes the programs and operating systems we need so we can use a computer.

Binary Code

When a person types on a keyboard, software converts the letters and numbers into a code that the computer can understand. This binary code consists of long strings of only two numbers, 0 and 1.

Whether the input to a software program on a computer is typed words, music or pictures, the role of the software is to eventually convert all this data into a binary code. A user who commands the software program to produce something, such as play a stored song, or open an email, is instructing the software to convert the binary code stored in files into an output that a human can easily understand, either through speakers or on the screen they are looking at.

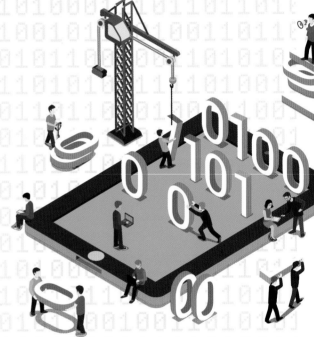

The Role of Software Programs

- Software programs are used to create, save, delete and open files.
- Some software is written just for one user, such as a business or a government department. Some software is written for users everywhere.
- Video games depend on software programmers and graphic designers to produce the exciting content that simulates reality.
- Cartoon movie producers use special graphics software to create the characters that attract moviegoers to cinemas.

Operating Systems

An operating system is the software on a computer that controls the type of other software and apps that can be loaded and used.

The main operating systems loaded onto computers around the world are:

- Microsoft Windows - used on PCs or personal computers
- Linux
- macOS - used on Apple computers and iOS used on Apple mobile devices such as iPhones and iPads
- Android - by Google
- Chrome OS - by Google

Programming Languages

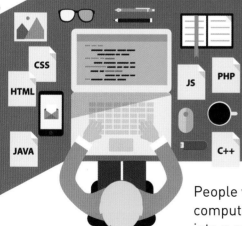

People who write software programs use one or more of many computer languages. These languages translate human requirements into a code a computer can act upon.

Some of the main computer languages are:

- HTML - used for Internet pages
- JavaScript - used for websites
- Perl - multipurpose
- C - one of the first computer languages
- Visual Basic - used with graphics
- SQL - used for searching databases
- Python - multipurpose
- Scratch - stories and games

How Does Software Get Into a Computer?

You can load computer software into a computer's hardware in a variety of ways:

1. Download via an Internet site
2. Copy from a disc
3. Copy from a USB flash drive
4. Use the cloud

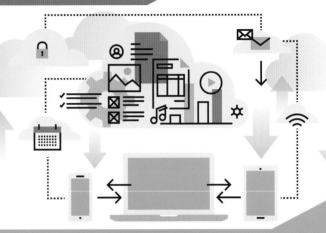

Cloud Software

'The Cloud' refers to computer software and data that a user accesses via the Internet. The user does not have to download all the software and data onto their own computer. As long as they have an Internet connection, they can access the cloud anywhere. Businesses that offer cloud services have their own computers in locations that may be in countries that are thousands of kilometres away from where the user is working.

ADVANTAGES OF THE CLOUD

- Can be less expensive than paying to download software
- User might only have to pay for the parts of the program they need
- User might pay a monthly fee instead of a large amount all at once
- Programs and data can be accessed in multiple locations and by many users

DISADVANTAGES OF THE CLOUD

- User depends on the provider to maintain their service and to stay in business
- Privacy and security of the information stored is a factor to consider

FLOPPY DISKS

Computer users sometimes used to load their new computer software from a floppy disk. Modern computers do not have a floppy disk slot, making all the old floppy disks unusable.

Installing New Software

After loading a new software program into a computer, you usually need to install it. Beware, as this is the stage at which viruses and malware can accidentally enter your computer. Read all the installation steps that show on the screen and only approve those that you really want to happen.

Is It User-Friendly?

Have you ever used new software on a computer and found it very difficult to understand? Software like this is not user-friendly. Computers exist to help humans at school, at home, at work and for recreation. If the software is not easy to navigate, the people who wrote the program and designed the graphics that appear on the screen have not thought enough about the computer ability of all the people who will be the users.

USER-FRIENDLY SOFTWARE FUNCTIONS

- Easy to navigate
- Main options clearly shown
- Simple descriptions of how it works
- Easy installation

USER-UNFRIENDLY SOFTWARE FUNCTIONS

- Updates have changed the screen location of important options
- Automatic Internet connection that uses up data
- Confusing error messages

Drivers

Hardware connected to a computer often needs a driver to make it work properly. A driver consists of code that allows a device, like a printer, to communicate with the computer. When new operating systems, such as Windows 10, first appear, the makers of hardware items usually need to update their driver software so that users' equipment will continue to work correctly.

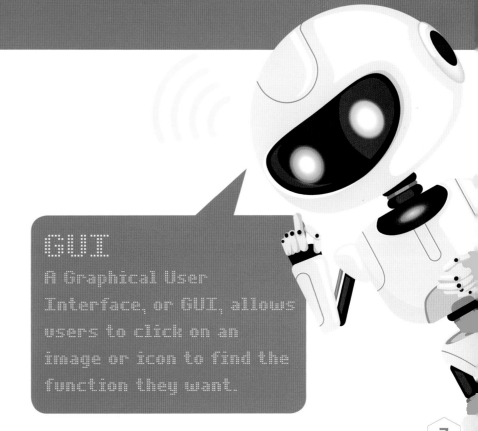

GUI

A Graphical User Interface, or GUI, allows users to click on an image or icon to find the function they want.

Viruses and Malware

Viruses and malware are software too. They are coded by people who want to be destructive or who have other criminal intentions. The word malware is short for malicious software. Often the user will not realise anything unwanted is loaded on their computer until they start experiencing problems with it.

How viruses and malware enter computers

- clicking on a link on a website
- clicking on a file attached to an email
- coping from a USB stick
- opening a shared file on a network
- opening a file received by Wi-Fi or Bluetooth

FIREWALL
The main purpose of a firewall is to prevent unauthorised access to a computer or network.

Antivirus Software

Businesses create antivirus software to protect computers from attack by viruses and malware. People who create the antivirus software understand many sorts of coding languages.

Software Updates and Patches

Updates and patches are usually provided when bugs or security vulnerabilities are identified, or to provide additional features to the software.

5 Ways to Avoid Viruses and Malware

1. Avoid clicking on suspicious email attachments or links

2. Avoid the big, blinking boxes on Internet sites that ask you to download

3. Avoid Internet sites offering free software, games and music that you normally have to pay for elsewhere

4. When installing software, read each step and do not tick to allow advertisements or other unwanted options

5. Only download from trusted sites

6. Use software updates and patches

The computer experts who write software are called programmers

People who want to become software programmers usually study a course in computing at a college or university.

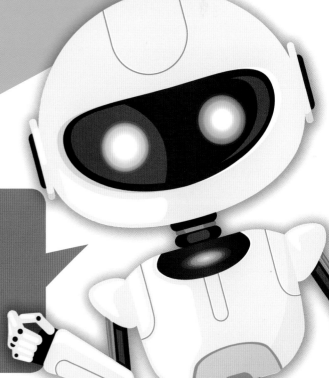

Data

Data is the information stored in a computer. One bit is the smallest piece of computer data that exists, consisting of either a 0 or a 1 in binary code. The word 'bit' is a shortened form of the words 'binary digit'. Eight bits together form one byte of data. Computers have limited amounts of data storage, measured in bytes.

8 bits	=	1 byte
1024 bytes	=	1 KB (a kilobyte stores about one typed page of words)
1024 KB	=	1 MB (a megabyte stores one about one photograph)
1024 MB	=	1 GB (a gigabyte stores about 200 songs)
1024 GB	=	1 TB (a terabyte stores about 250 movies)

Database

A database is a collection of data that needs software to make it easy for a human to use. A database usually contains rows and columns of information, as in a Microsoft Excel spreadsheet.

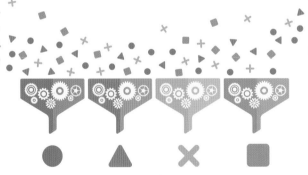

Big Data

Big Data refers to databases that are extremely large. Governments and businesses are the main users and creators of Big Data databases.

Big Data needs computers that have the power to store the information, and to run the special software that allows a user to access it.

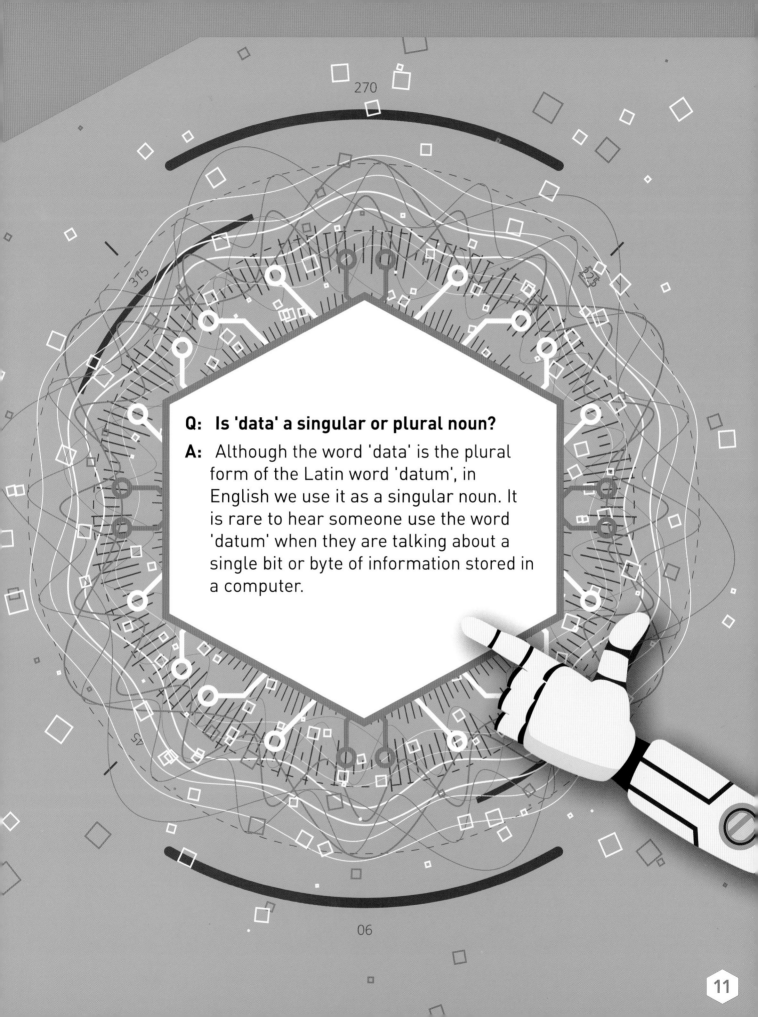

Q: **Is 'data' a singular or plural noun?**

A: Although the word 'data' is the plural form of the Latin word 'datum', in English we use it as a singular noun. It is rare to hear someone use the word 'datum' when they are talking about a single bit or byte of information stored in a computer.

Files and Folders

Files are the places where computer users store their data. Files names have different endings or extensions depending on the sort of software that created them.

File Extension	Software Program	Main Purpose
.docx	Word	typed documents
.xlsx	Excel	data in tables and columns
.jpeg	graphics software	pictures
.mrc	MARC software	describing books in libraries
.pdf	Adobe Acrobat	documents that do not allow overwriting

Files are not actually part of a computer's software. Files are called computer assets or resources instead.

If you only have a few files, storing them on the desktop is a quick way to find them again. If you have lots of files, it is much better to create folders and store files on the same subject together in their own folder. For example, create a folder called 'Pets' for pictures of your cat and dog. Then create another file called 'Volcanoes' for your homework project on volcanoes. Doing this will help to make finding all your files much easier.

Computer folders are the digital version of the cardboard folders that workers use in offices to store and separate their paperwork. This is why the Microsoft icon for a folder looks like a cardboard folder.

Saving Files

Get into the habit of saving files frequently while you are working on them. Avoid waiting until you are finished with a file before you save it. If the computer crashes, or there is a power failure, you may lose all your work if it is unsaved.

When you first save a file, a message usually appears asking where you want to save the file. Choose an easy-to-find location so that you can open the file quickly the next time you need it. The default location that the computer selects may not always be the best one for your needs.

Backup

Backup refers to copying a file to an external hard drive, either on another computer, a USB stick, some other portable drive or a cloud storage service. Backup should happen frequently to avoid losing all files if the computer crashes.

HANDY TIP

If you need to backup a file but do not have anything to copy it to, email it to someone you trust. You can then get a copy of it from them later.

Passwords for Files

To protect a file from being opened by someone else, most software allows users to add a password to it. Be sure to use a password that is easy to remember or you will not be able to open the file again.

Recycle Bin

When a computer user deletes a file, it does not immediately disappear from the hardware. The file goes to the Recycle Bin where it stays until the user chooses to delete it. This is a safety feature as it allows the retrieval of a file that has been deleted by mistake. To free up space in a computer's storage, delete the contents of the Recycle Bin regularly.

Software in Industry

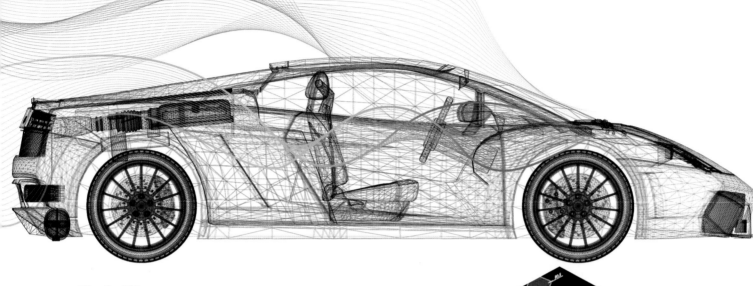

CAD

CAD, or Computer Aided Design, uses software programs in the design of buildings, cars, mechanical parts and many other technical items. Before computer software existed to produce these design drawings, people used Technical Drawing, which involved drawing scale diagrams for engineers to use when making mechanical items or constructing buildings. These drawing were called blueprints, a name which is still used for the printout from a CAD software program.

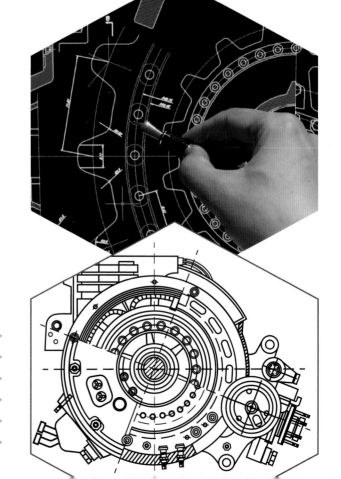

Finances

Businesses use accounting software programs to record all their financial information. The developments in software for accounting have resulted in the loss of jobs which involved counting, adding and writing figures in large books called ledgers. Data entry operators have taken over these roles in offices.

Accounting software has developed to be able to produce full taxation and financial information, without a person having to tally up days of sales and purchasing data before knowing the state of an organisation's finances.

People who want to keep track of their own private spending also use accounting software to run their family's finances and make sure they are not spending too much on things they do not really need.

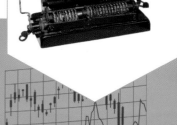

History of Accounting Aids

4,000 years ago	Abacus
400 years ago	Slide rule
400 years ago	Mechanical calculator
50 years ago	Electric desktop calculator
40 years ago	Hand-held calculators
40 years ago	Accounting software for personal computers

...ial report

...lance sheet

Assets 1,734,826
Current assets 88,905
Non-current assets 1,645,921

Liabilities 166,630
Current liabilities 110,327
Non-current liabilities 56,303

Equity 74,393
Paid-in capital 72,921
Retained earnings 1,472

Income statement

Revenues 12,978,516
Net sales 12,873,892
Investment 104,624

Expenses 6,372,535
Research and Development 1,385,395
Operating expenses 4,439,118
Marketing 548,022

Net income 6,505,981

Equity statement

Current year 1,774,576
Comprehensive income 15,897
Issue of share capital 88,905
Dividends 23,853

Previous year 166,630
Comprehensive income 110,327
Issue of share capital 56,303
Dividends 67,676

...ash flow statement

...erations 12,978,516
...earnings 12,873,892
...reciation 104,624

...vesting 6,372,535
...eal estate 1,385,395
...uipment 4,439,118

...ing 6,505,981
6,505,981

85%   65%

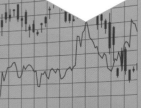

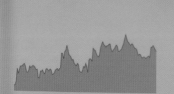

100 | ☢ | 8888

LEVEL
88

♥ | 10

$ 8888888

x 8.8

8888

Gaming Software

The creation of computer and video gaming software is a large, international industry. The original computer games involved moving a symbol around a basic grid layout, but the software for games has now moved far beyond this. Game developers now need to study many programming languages and be able to construct complex algorithms.

Writing gaming software can be a career goal for people who understand computer languages and the creation of software.

MENU

Mission display HUD.

ANTI-PROTON
GUN
1000

PLASMA
MISSILE
50

Interview With a Game Developer

Kris is an Australian video game programmer. He loved playing computer games as a child and now makes his own. He attended the Academy of Interactive Entertainment where he studied Game Programming.

....INTERVIEW WITH KRIS

INTERVIEWER: Tell me about video games production.

KRIS: *To produce a video game, we need an artist to create the art of the game, a designer to have the idea and to work out the specifics of the gameplay, and a programmer to make it function.*

INTERVIEWER: What do you have to do to become a video game programmer?

KRIS: *To become a video game programmer you need to have an understanding of how coding works. I started off by teaching myself to create games while in primary school, using free programs such as Klik'n'Play and Scratch.*

Then, in secondary school, I was introduced to a tool called Unity 3D, and I used that to make more advanced games.

INTERVIEWER: What computer languages and programs did you need to learn about?

KRIS: *Many programming languages look similar and do similar things. They all let you define the value of things (like the height of a ball), do maths on those values (like calculate how fast it falls due to gravity), and test when something important happens (like the ball hits the ground).*

Beginner tools like Scratch use a graphical code editor. More advanced tools, like Unity 3D, can use languages such as JavaScript or C# in their programs, and you type those with a text editor.

Graphics Software

Graphics software allows graphic artists and designers to create images that look realistic, or pictures that look like drawings or paintings. Photos taken by digital cameras can look better or even completely different after being changed or enhanced by graphics software.

Artists create digital images using software that imitates the use of pens, pencils and paint brushes. After printing, the final work of art can hang on a wall, or appear in advertising or on a website.

ADVERTISING

Advertising departments in large businesses often employ many graphic designers and artists, all working on making consumer products look amazing online, on television, in magazines or on billboards beside roads.

MOVIES

Graphics software is an important tool used in the movie industry to create cartoons and background scenery. It also allows actors to perform stunts that would be too dangerous or even impossible to do in reality.

Graphics and Binary Code

The role of graphics software is to change the images that a user creates on a computer screen into a code that a computer can understand. All digital images are stored as binary code, which is a sequence of the numbers 0 and 1.

Graphics and Pixels

Computers display images as a collection of tiny squares called pixels. Zooming in to an image on a screen will reveal these tiny dots, each made up of one colour.

Computers store data about images in a table and show the image on a grid of pixels. The pixel colour depends on the coding behind it.

BITMAP

The data that a computer reads to produce an image is called a bitmap.

RESOLUTION

Images with a lot of pixels are called high resolution, and those with few pixels are called low resolution. A low resolution image has rough edges, poor colour and little detail. Pixelated is a term used to describe these types of images.

Software in Cars

Car owners with an interest in mechanics used to be able to repair and service their cars themselves. Now that so many of a car's functions use computer software, an expert who understands computers is often the only person who can make sure a repair or adjustment is safe. Rather than looking for a part that is broken, mechanics can sometimes access the car's computer to find out what is not working properly.

Some cars might also connect to the manufacturer via the Internet, sending and receiving data about performance and problems.

Driverless Cars

Driverless cars depend on computer software to allow them to navigate to a location while avoiding collisions and keeping within lane markings on the road. Software might also control the fuel usage, turn wiper blades or lights on and off, or check on the tyre pressure.

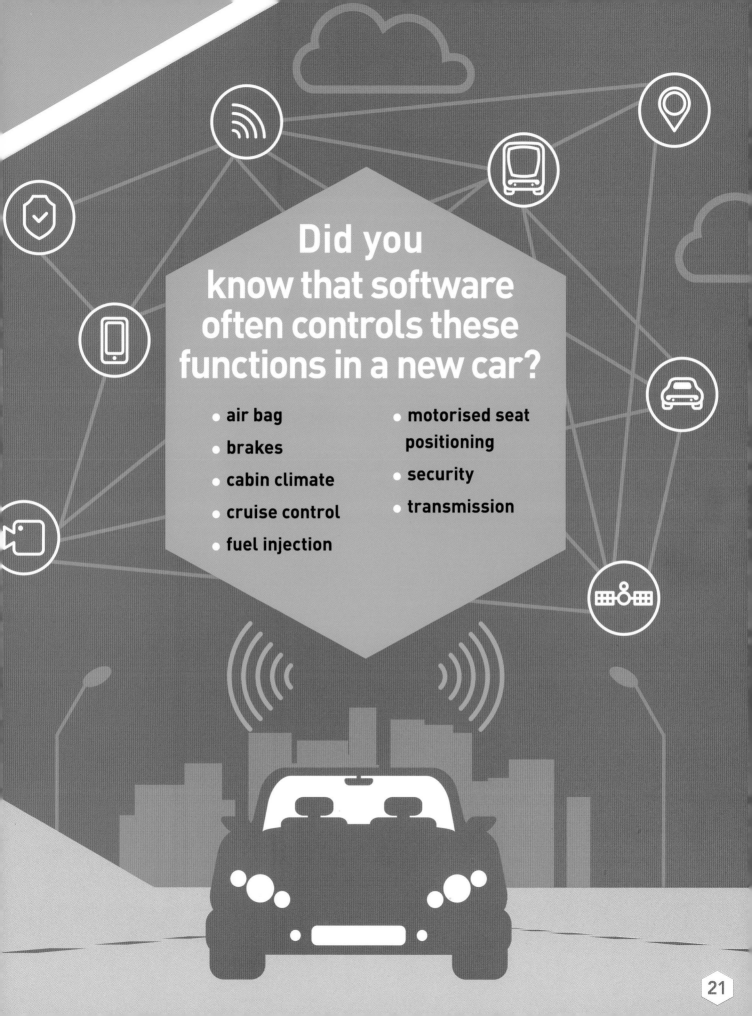

Did you know that software often controls these functions in a new car?

- air bag
- brakes
- cabin climate
- cruise control
- fuel injection

- motorised seat positioning
- security
- transmission

Apps

The word app is short for application. An app is software used on mobile devices such as tablets and mobile phones. Some programs that run on a laptop or a desktop computer are also called apps.

Apps have different structures depending on whether they are for use on an Android or Apple device. A user goes to a different online source to locate the app they want for their type of device.

Some apps are free and some are sold for varying amounts of money. To use an app that is not free, you will need to have an account with an app store or provider.

Do You Want to Create Apps?

People who create apps are called app developers. They design apps for a business they work for, or they might place their own apps on the various app stores and receive payment when people choose to download them.

Software for Kids

Software for children includes resources used at school or for learning at home, as well as games for recreation.

SCHOOL SOFTWARE

Some school lessons depend on software to show students the subjects being taught in class, and then to rate their performance on quizzes. Children can also use software at home to help them with homework, or provide extra activities for students who want to know more.

GAMES AND LEARNING

While computer games can become addictive, they are also a great way for children to learn how to use a keyboard, think quickly and develop hand-eye coordination.

Emails

Email programs are part of a computer's software. The worldwide popularity of emails has resulted in a decline in the use of letters, or 'snail mail', as people choose the more instant communication that email allows.

The First Emails

The first messages between computers did not use the Internet. They were sent in the 1960s amongst a private group of computers. The general public started using emails in the 1980s, when businesses began setting up servers which could control the flow of emails between users who were not a part of any private computer network.

How Do Emails Work?

An email is composed of data which travels to an email server. The data sits on the server until the receiver downloads it. The data travels as binary code which is then translated by software into what the email user sees on their screen.

Email Safety

- Hackers have invented ways to intercept emails to find out what people are writing about to each other.

- Cyber criminals use emails to persuade people to open files that contain software which damages files.

- Bullies use emails to upset people or to spread harmful gossip.

JUNK MAIL
Email software usually offers users an option to mark unwanted email as Junk. Doing this instructs the computer not to show any email from the same address again. Cyber criminals get around this restriction by frequently changing the email address they use.

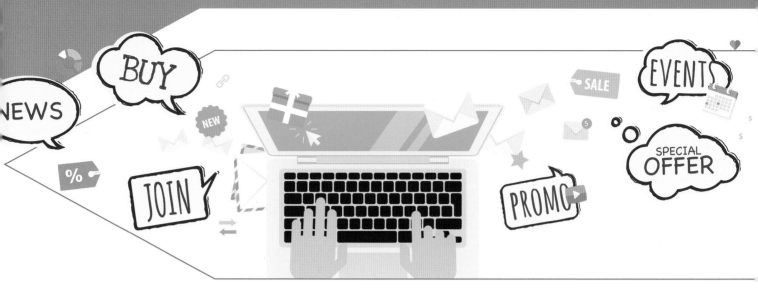

Email Marketing

Businesses use emails to send advertising to their customers. Email users often wonder how a business has obtained their email address when they have never been in contact with them before. If you have ever given your email address as part of a promotion, to obtain a store loyalty card, or to access a website, your email address can later be sold to different businesses without your knowledge. If your email address is on a website or social media site, people you do not know can easily access it and add it to their list.

Sometimes email marketing provides a useful service, letting you know about sales or products that are of interest to you, or offering special prices or events that are only available to members of a club or group. Email advertising should include a link that allows the receiver to unsubscribe.

POP or IMAP?

Emails are set up using a POP or IMAP protocol. POP stands for Post Office Protocol. It allows emails to download to your own computer. IMAP stands for Internet Message Access Protocol. It allows emails to stay on the service provider so that you can access and synchronise them anywhere with an Internet enabled device, such as a mobile phone, computer or tablet.

@

In the 1970s, Ray Tomlinson became the first person to use the @ symbol in email addresses.

Social Media Software

Social media such as Facebook, Snapchat, Instagram and Twitter all use software of various types. These businesses constantly update their software to make their product more interesting for users. They also use software to create the advertising they use to generate their business income.

ALGORITHMS

The algorithms used by social media are designed to make the user's online experience relevant to them by showing information that is often based on their previous searching history or on their location. Algorithms also control the blocking of unwanted content and are all written using software.

Music
Software

LISTENING TO MUSIC

Music software has changed the way people enjoy listening to their favourite songs and instrumentals. In the late 1900s, portable CD players were the most popular way to listen to music when people were travelling, jogging or relaxing in the outdoors. Small digitised music players have replaced the CD for most people. A CD held about twelve songs, but a Wi-Fi connected digital player has access to thousands.

CREATING MUSIC

The use of digital software to record music has allowed entertainers who are starting their career to create their own recordings and make them available on the Internet, where millions of people can hear them.

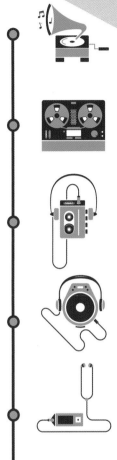

DAW (Digital Audio Workstation)
Software

Performers who want to produce their own music files will need to use some form of DAW software. There are many types available, ranging from basic for beginners up to complex for professionals.

Microsoft produces software used around the world by children for their homework or by adults in households, businesses and governments. While there are many other software creators, Microsoft is one of the leaders in the field.

Microsoft Shortcuts

To use these shortcuts in a Microsoft document, first highlight the line or text you want to work with, and then hold down the CTRL key while pressing the letter key. Finally, release both keys.

CTRL A	Select All	CTRL P	Print
CTRL B	Bold	CTRL R	Right Align
CTRL C	Copy	CTRL S	Save
CTRL E	Centre Align	CTRL U	Underline
CTRL END	Go To End of Document	CTRL V	Paste
CTRL HOME	Go To Top of Document	CTRL Y	Repeat Last Action
CTRL I	Italic	CTRL Z	Undo Last Action

How to Create a Column Graph in Excel

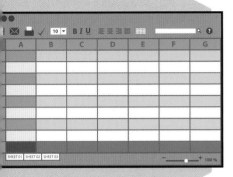

To create a graph in Excel, you first need to enter some data into cells in a spreadsheet. A spreadsheet has columns named by letters across the top and by numbers down the left hand side. Each cell is identified by its location on the grid. The first cell is called A1 and the cell beneath it is called A2.

TO CREATE A COLUMN GRAPH SHOWING
THE TEMPERATURE ON 5 DAYS OF THE WEEK:

1. Open Microsoft Excel

2. Enter the names of the days of the week in column A.

3. Enter the temperatures in column B.

4. Highlight the data you have entered.

5. Find the Charts options in the Toolbar.

6. Choose one of the display options to create the chart.

7. A graph appears on your screen.

8. Click on the chart's borders and find CHART TOOLS in the Toolbar at the top.

9. Experiment with the options in the Toolbar to find out how to change the colours and layout of the graph you have created.

10. To copy the chart and past it into another document, move the cursor over the chart border until the cross-hairs appear. Then right click and select Copy from the list of commands that appears.

TIP:

In different versions of Excel, the locations of Toolbar options may be slightly different.

Microsoft Word

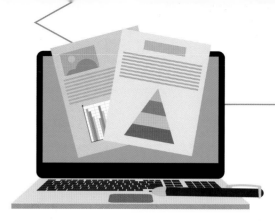

How to resize an image that is too large or too small

1. Click on the image in Word so that its corners are displayed.

2. Move the cursor to one of the four corners and stop when you see a double headed arrow.

3. Click on the arrow and drag inwards or outwards to resize the image.

4. Do not click on one of the sides of the image or there will be distortion when you drag to resize.

How to make part of an image transparent so that you can see whatever is underneath it on the page

1. Click on the image in the Word document.

2. Find the picture formatting Toolbar.

3. Find the tiny arrow next to the word **Recolor**.

4. From the drop-down box click on **Set Transparent Color**. (Your cursor turns into a tiny pen symbol.)

5. Move the symbol over the colour you want to be transparent in the image and click. (You can only make one colour transparent at a time.)

Tech Terms for Kids

algorithm	coding that gives a set of instructions to a computer
Android	operating system used by non-Apple devices
app	software used on mobile devices
backup	copying data to a safe location away from the main computer
Big Data	very large database
bit	binary digit
bitmap	table that a computer reads to create an image on the screen
Bluetooth	short range radio connection
byte	eight bits
CAD	Computer Aided Design
cloud	software and data storage available via the Internet
database	information stored on a computer, usually in tabular form
DAW	Digital Audio Workstation
default	option in software setup chosen by the developers
download	copy from an outside source to a computer's hard drive
driver	software that allows a device and a computer to interact
file extension	ending letters of a file name after the period
firewall	used to secure a computer or network and block unauthorised access
format images	alter images

graphics	images
GUI	Graphical User Interface
junk email	unwanted email that is blocked from appearing
malware	malicious software
navigate	find out how to use a software program
patch	coding that updates software and makes it safer or easier to use
pixel	smallest element of an image
pixelated image	low resolution image
POP / IMAP	ways of accessing emails
programmer	person who creates software
protocol	rules for running a system
resolution	based on the number of pixels in an image
server	computer that stores large amounts of data or software code and allows other networked computers access
simulate	pretend to be something
snail mail	sending real letters through the postal service
spreadsheet	table produced by a program such as Excel
synchronise	allow a group of Internet enabled devices to share recent data so they are all up-to-date
user-friendly	easy to understand
virus	software that damages computers
Wi-Fi	wireless network

31

Index